DAWN

AN ADVENT DEVOTIONAL

Published by Dwell
Design by Gabriel Reyes-Ordeix

Dwell

AN ADVENT DEVOTIONAL

DAWN

Contents

<u>Introduction</u>

"Weeping may
tarry for the
night, but joy
comes with
the morning."

Ps 30:5

THROUGHOUT SCRIPTURE, beginning with the first chapter of Genesis, we are invited into a story of darkness and light. Our world is filled with beauty and wonder, as well as sickness and sorrow. This is seen on a universal scale and is encountered within the hidden places of every human heart. In truth, life is neither complete darkness nor perpetual light, at least on this side of eternity.

We live in a world that knows the darkness of night yet has been forever transformed by the light of Christ that ushers in the dawn.

Advent invites us to journey through the darkness to discover the light, the incarnate Word of God who "shines in the darkness, and the darkness has not overcome it" (John 1:5). Though darkness may press in on every side, threatening to overwhelm, we cling to the joy that comes with the morning, for Christ is with us. In the timeless words of *Silent Night*, this Advent, let us rejoice afresh in "the dawn of redeeming grace."

And so, we look *back* to the birth of Christ that forever filled our world with the light of life, yet Advent is also an opportunity to explore the *present* with an eye to the *future*. Where is your life most overcome by darkness, and how can a living encounter with the incarnate Christ fill you with hope and a deeper longing for his return?

As you journey through the Advent season with this devotional as a guide, you will be invited daily to focus your entire being—mind, soul, and strength—on the light of Christ as revealed in Scripture. You will hear classic wisdom from men and women who have gone ahead of us, bearing witness to the light as it transformed their own lives. And through the prayers and reflective practices, you are invited not simply to *think* about the light of Christ but to open your life to his transforming grace, to set your eyes on the eastern horizon and look with expectancy for "the bright morning star" (Rev 22:16).

First Week *of* Advent

Surely his salvation is near to those who
fear him, that glory may dwell in our land.
Ps 85:9

"There is a birth from God before the ages, and a birth from a virgin at the fullness of time. There is a hidden coming, like that of rain on fleece, and a coming before all eyes, still in the future."

-St. Cyril of Jerusalem

A Hidden Coming

 OPEN DWELL AND LISTEN TO
Isaiah 64:1–9; Psalm 80:1–7, 17–19;
1 Corinthians 1:3–9; Mark 13:24–37

THIS TIME OF YEAR, our culture is bathed in the warm glow of holiday lights. Even the most hardened skeptic's resolve is tested by a steady stream of nostalgic films, music, meals, and customs, and at the center of this sentimentality lies a baby in a manger. At the mention of this babe, it is difficult to think of anything other than the traditional nativity scene with Mary, Joseph, Wise Men, and a smattering of barn-yard animals all reverently paying tribute to the newborn king. Timeless as this picture may be, it is an incomplete and one-sided understanding of the nature and purpose of Christ's birth.

In Advent, we see both the humility and the power of God on display. In Christ, we encounter God entering our world's chaos and brokenness and taking it upon himself to heal, redeem, and restore. Yet simultaneously, it is a birth that shakes the earth to its very core. The same power that tears the veil in two, splits rocks, and opens tombs is contained in the frailty and vulnerability of an infant child (Matt 27:51-53).

Jesus' birth definitively answers the prayer of Isaiah 64:1: "Oh that you would rend the heavens and come down, that the mountains might quake at your presence." Advent literally means "coming" or "approach," and as the people of God, we are invited every year to enter attentively into a season of holy anticipation. As we do, let us never lose sight of the true nature of the king that came and will come again.

PRAYER for THE WEEK

Almighty God, give us grace to cast away the works of darkness, and put on the armor of light, now in the time of this mortal life in which your Son Jesus Christ came to visit us in great humility; that in the last day, when he shall come again in his glorious majesty to judge both the living and the dead, we may rise to the life immortal; through him who lives and reigns with you and the Holy Spirit, one God, now and for ever. *Amen.*

REFLECTIVE PRACTICE

In a season filled with busyness and distraction, this week, you are invited to focus on the practice of **prayer**. To begin, reflect today on where you pray.

Do you have a dedicated place of prayer in your home?

Creating a reverent space for God in our homes reflects our desire to cultivate a heart of worship and devotion. Matching our homes to our hearts in this way helps to orient the whole of our lives toward Christ this Advent season.

NOTES

"It is true that sin is cause
of all this pain; but all shall
be well, and all shall be well,
and all manner of thing
shall be well."

-Julian of Norwich

All Shall Be Well

 OPEN DWELL AND LISTEN TO
*Psalm 79; Micah 4:1-5;
Revelation 15:1-8*

ADVENT FORCES US TO CONFRONT our brokenness within and the chaos without. Though it defies contemporary logic, sin is a sickness for which we cannot find a lasting cure. No amount of technological advancement or scientific inquiry will yield a solution to this timeless problem. For this reason, Advent developed in the Church as a penitential season of preparation. As God draws near, we are invited to grieve the way sin alienates us from Christ and one another. We acknowledge our need for the mercy and compassion of our Lord. As the Psalmist cries out, "Help us, O God of our salvation, for the glory of your name; deliver us, and atone for our sins, for your name's sake!" (Ps 79:9).

Themes of light and darkness feature heavily in the Scripture readings during this season. In the ancient world, electricity and artificial light were foreign concepts. Instead, in Scripture, we frequently encounter images of the fiery presence of God. It is this wild and untamable light that pierces even the deepest darkness. It is a fire that consumes and burns as it draws near. And, as confusing as it may seem at first, this is profoundly good news!

Christians are meant to be aflame with the life of God. Like the burning bush of old, we are invited to be filled with the fire of God yet not consumed or destroyed by it. The approaching fire of God is meant for our healing, never our harm. The Lord loves us more than we know how to love ourselves, and as we open to the healing flame of his love, we rest in the promise that all shall be well.

PRAYER for THE WEEK

Almighty God, give us grace to cast away
the works of darkness, and put on the
armor of light, now in the time of this
mortal life in which your Son Jesus Christ
came to visit us in great humility; that in
the last day, when he shall come again
in his glorious majesty to judge both the
living and the dead, we may rise to the
life immortal; through him who lives and
reigns with you and the Holy Spirit,
one God, now and for ever. *Amen.*

REFLECTIVE PRACTICE

Just as we reflected yesterday on where we pray,
today we consider when we pray.

While we can and should pray anywhere and always,
our life with God is strengthened when we establish
intentional and predictable patterns of prayer.

None of this needs to be heroic. Starting very small,
even with a single minute of prayer, can till the soil
of our hearts, creating intimate space for God's
love to grow.

NOTES

"You seek a happy life in
a land of the dying: it is not
there. How could a life be
happy where life is missing?
Our life, our true Life,
descended into the world,
took our death upon his back
and destroyed it with the
superabundance of his life."

-St. Augustine of Hippo

True Happiness

 OPEN DWELL AND LISTEN TO
Psalm 79; Micah 4:6–13;
Revelation 18:1–10

ADVENT IS FUNDAMENTALLY A JOURNEY OF LOVE. In this sense, it is a season of heightened attentiveness, reminding us of what is true in every time and every place. It is the love of God that draws near in Christ, the Spirit of God that nourishes and sustains us along our way, and perfect union with God the Father that remains the aim and destination of our lives. And while we know this to be true in the core of our being, life is often lived shortsighted. We are easily distracted, pulled to one side or the other by lesser loves that promise fulfillment yet leave us hollow and disfigured.

To encounter the love of God this Advent season, you must be willing to turn away from the desires that leave you spiritually blind and numb. As Revelation reminds us, we live in a world like Babylon of old–drunk on sexual desire, power, and luxury. The solution? "Come out of her, my people, lest you take part in her sins, lest you share in her plagues." (Rev 18:4).

True happiness is not found in absolute freedom but in a life aligned with the virtues and values of the kingdom of God. The ways of the Lord are never for your harm but for your renewal and restoration. You are set free to receive a love that makes you truly human, a love that so transforms your heart and mind that you are sent, turned outward to give your life away as a gift of love for the life of the world. This is the true spirit of Advent and where happiness is always to be found.

PRAYER for THE WEEK

Almighty God, give us grace to cast away
the works of darkness, and put on the
armor of light, now in the time of this
mortal life in which your Son Jesus Christ
came to visit us in great humility; that in
the last day, when he shall come again
in his glorious majesty to judge both the
living and the dead, we may rise to the
life immortal; through him who lives and
reigns with you and the Holy Spirit,
one God, now and for ever. *Amen.*

REFLECTIVE PRACTICE

As you continue to explore where and when
you pray, remember that it is always possible
to designate a space and carve out time, and yet
it's entirely natural to feel inattentive and distant.

Work to let all of those feelings fall away and
simply be as present as you can. We all have
to learn to crawl before we walk.

NOTES

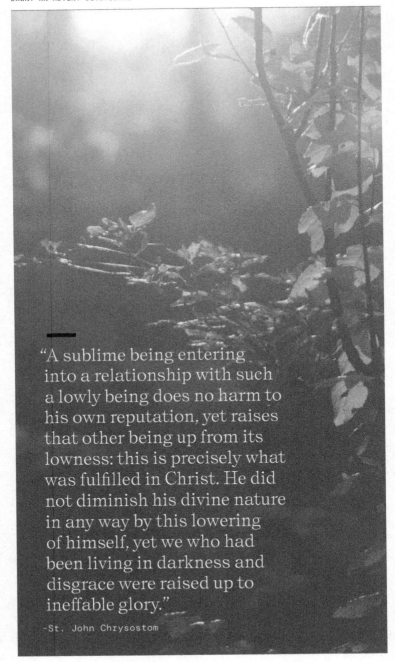

"A sublime being entering into a relationship with such a lowly being does no harm to his own reputation, yet raises that other being up from its lowness: this is precisely what was fulfilled in Christ. He did not diminish his divine nature in any way by this lowering of himself, yet we who had been living in darkness and disgrace were raised up to ineffable glory."

-St. John Chrysostom

Humble Glory

 OPEN DWELL AND LISTEN TO
Psalm 79; Micah 5:1–5a;
Luke 21:34–38

AT THE HEART OF THE CHRISTIAN FAITH lies the belief that
God sees, loves, and welcomes the forgotten, the marginali-
zed, and the downhearted. In a world that values and cele-
brates the strong and powerful, time and time again, in word
and deed, Jesus reminds us that weakness and humility are
the way to glory and the path of lasting peace. In this way,
Advent is a persistent reminder of the upside-down nature
of God's kingdom.

The lowliness of the Incarnation was foretold long ago.
As Micah reminds us, it is from Bethlehem, "one of the
little clans of Judah," that the true king of Israel will come,
one who "shall stand and shepherd his flock in the strength
of the LORD (Mic 5:2, 4). From these humble origins, Jesus
continues to invite us to tend to what is often overlooked,
neglected, and undervalued. Do not be weighed down by the
worries of this life (Luke 21:34), but learn to see the glory of
God breaking in all around you. It is the mustard seed that
grows to give shade and rest to all who draw near (Matt
13:31–32). It is yeast, small and unseen, that leavens the
entire loaf (Luke 13:20–21).

In a season filled with countless distractions and sources
of potential stress, it is easy to ignore the humble hope of
Advent and the tender compassion of our Lord. Similarly,
we may be tempted to believe that the cares of life are of
little interest to our Lord. Surely, he has more important
things demanding his time and attention! Yet in the quiet
humility of the manger in Bethlehem, we are reminded
once again that not a single concern goes unnoticed,
not a sorrow left unhealed.

PRAYER for THE WEEK

Almighty God, give us grace to cast away
the works of darkness, and put on the
armor of light, now in the time of this
mortal life in which your Son Jesus Christ
came to visit us in great humility; that in
the last day, when he shall come again
in his glorious majesty to judge both the
living and the dead, we may rise to the
life immortal; through him who lives and
reigns with you and the Holy Spirit,
one God, now and for ever. *Amen.*

REFLECTIVE PRACTICE

The words we use in prayer reveal our assumptions
about God and how we relate to him. For this
reason, Jesus teaches us that God is "Our Father,"
first and foremost.

Perhaps you could try a similar prayer today: "Abba,
I belong to you." You may consider repeating that
phrase for a single minute. For, as the saints of old
tell us, repetition is the mother of all learning.

NOTES

"Repentance itself is nothing
but a kind of circling: to turn
to the One by repentance
from whom, by sin,
we have turned away."

-Lancelot Andrewes

Let Us Return

 OPEN DWELL AND LISTEN TO
Psalm 85:1-2, 8-13; Hosea 6:1-6;
1 Thessalonians 1:2-10

TO LIVE AS A CHRISTIAN, one must learn to be comfortable with tension. Though it is not as simple as we prefer, wisdom is found in holding seemingly contradictory ideas close to one another. Take, for example, the ancient words given to us today from Hosea 6:1: "Come, let us return to the LORD." Within this single phrase, we are confronted with the reality of our own initiative and responsibility to tend to our life with God, as well as the fact that any genuine return to God is first made possible by his movement toward us.

In Advent, as our Lord draws near, we must actively examine the condition of our lives. Are we ready to greet him upon his arrival? In this way, repentance always lies at the heart of faithful preparation. To repent is to not only feel sorrow over the effect of sin in your heart and life but is equally an act of the will, purposefully turning away from sin and death and taking on habits that lead us into places of peace.

You can passionately pursue God without falling into the trap of anxious toil or self-assured living. In fact, the Incarnation of God is the end of all striving. As we "press on to know the LORD" (Hos 6:3), we do so knowing that it is God in Christ Jesus who heals us, raises us up, and makes us whole. Advent reminds us that we have work to do, inviting us to take seriously the call to holy and faithful living. Yet this way of life is not of our making. It is a gift to be received, like spring rain that falls to water the parched earth.

PRAYER for THE WEEK

Almighty God, give us grace to cast away
the works of darkness, and put on the
armor of light, now in the time of this
mortal life in which your Son Jesus Christ
came to visit us in great humility; that in
the last day, when he shall come again
in his glorious majesty to judge both the
living and the dead, we may rise to the
life immortal; through him who lives and
reigns with you and the Holy Spirit,
one God, now and for ever. *Amen.*

REFLECTIVE PRACTICE

Prayer invites us into a conversation with God,
not a one-way monologue. As we grow in our life
of prayer, we therefore must also grow in our
willingness to listen to God.

Consider making your prayer today one single
minute of silence.

NOTES

"I beg and beseech you, Lord: grant to all who have gone astray a true knowledge of you, so that each and every one may come to know your glory."

-St. Isaac the Syrian

True Knowledge

 OPEN DWELL AND LISTEN TO
*Psalm 85:1–2, 8–13; Jeremiah 1:4–10;
Acts 11:19–26*

IN KEEPING WITH ST. PAUL'S WORDS in Romans 12:2, Christians in every age are invited to be "transformed by the renewal of the mind." Yet, as people who live on this side of the printing press (not to mention the internet or the iPhone), how are we to understand these ancient words when endless mental stimulation and information lie just a few swipes or clicks away? While the mind can and should be renewed, it must never be isolated from the *holistic* transformation that is envisioned in and through the Incarnation.

Jesus took on the fullness of humanity so that humanity in its fullness could be redeemed. We must never forget: God wants to be known! As the Psalms remind us today, though we have all gone astray and live in self-made exile, our Lord, in his kindness, speaks to us and makes us able to hear (Ps 85:8). True knowledge of God is never the abstract acquisition of facts but an embodied encounter with the living Christ.

Cliché as it may sound, we must remember that it is possible to live with a wealth of information about God without ever encountering his living presence. Faith must never be reduced to a mental pursuit. Advent teaches us that God loves his creatures *in their creatureliness*, so much so that he takes human nature upon himself. Every sense given to you is a gift from God that can lead you closer to him as you journey from this life into glory.

PRAYER for THE WEEK

Almighty God, give us grace to cast away
the works of darkness, and put on the
armor of light, now in the time of this
mortal life in which your Son Jesus Christ
came to visit us in great humility; that in
the last day, when he shall come again
in his glorious majesty to judge both the
living and the dead, we may rise to the
life immortal; through him who lives and
reigns with you and the Holy Spirit,
one God, now and for ever. *Amen.*

REFLECTIVE PRACTICE

Sometimes in life, we need physical reminders
that draw us out of our minds and into the world
around us. Today you are invited to include your
senses in this week's habit of prayer.

As you pray, consider engaging your sense of smell
with a lit candle, or your sense of sight by placing
an image of Christ nearby. Or, mix up your routine
and go for a walk in nature, giving thanks to
God for the beauty and wonder of his creation.

NOTES

"Maintain the conviction that our disorderliness is not natural to us, and do not listen to those who say, 'It is no use talking about it, because that is just how we are made, and you cannot do anything about it.' That is not how we are made, and if we undertake to cure ourselves, then we will be able to do something about it."

-St. Theophan the Recluse

Becoming Human

 OPEN DWELL AND LISTEN TO
Psalm 85:1-2, 8-13; Ezekiel 36:24-28;
Mark 11:27-33

TO LIVE AS A FOLLOWER OF JESUS is to believe that transformation is possible. It is to profess through word and deed that we are not finished products, and our journey has not reached its destination. Whatever keeps you up at night or leaves you anxious during the day does not have to forever define who you are or who you will be. Yet, it is remarkably easy to fall into this way of thinking, is it not? "I've always been this way," we say, throwing our hands up in defeat. Though common and understandable, we must begin to see that there is nothing inherently Christian about this way of viewing the world or our place within it.

It is possible to live your entire life and never become truly human. In many ways, this is one of the primary insights we are meant to glean from this season of preparation. Though we may eat, sleep, laugh, and cry, in the process we are capable of missing the end for which we were created: namely, to share in the very life of God. In taking on flesh and bones, Jesus condescends and speaks to us "at our level." Yet the heart of his message was, is, and will forever be one of growth, becoming something we previously were not.

As God promises in Ezekiel 36:26, "I will remove the heart of stone from your flesh and give you a heart of flesh." Fundamentally, this is a promise of transformation. It is a reminder that we can live without being truly alive. In short, it is an invitation to become fully human.

PRAYER *for* THE WEEK

Almighty God, give us grace to cast away
the works of darkness, and put on the
armor of light, now in the time of this
mortal life in which your Son Jesus Christ
came to visit us in great humility; that in
the last day, when he shall come again
in his glorious majesty to judge both the
living and the dead, we may rise to the
life immortal; through him who lives and
reigns with you and the Holy Spirit,
one God, now and for ever. *Amen.*

REFLECTIVE PRACTICE

To wrap up this week's focus on prayer,
today we invite you to reflect on your experience.
What resonated? Where did you notice resistance?
Consider putting your thoughts in a journal.

A simple record of your life with God can serve
as a source of great encouragement, showing
you where you've been and, more significantly,
who you're becoming.

NOTES

Second Week *of* Advent

Wait for the Lord; be strong, and let your heart
take courage; wait for the Lord!
Ps 27:14

"Where there is no fear, in like manner there is no amendment; where there is no amendment, repentance is of necessity vain, for it lacks the fruit for which God sowed it; that is, man's salvation."

-Tertullian

Pointing to Christ

 OPEN DWELL AND LISTEN TO
Isaiah 40:1–11; Psalm 85:1–2, 8–13; 2 Peter 3:8–15a; Mark 1:1–8

HAVE YOU EVER LOOKED at an ancient icon or historic Christian painting and struggled to tell what was happening? If so, you're in good company! While appreciating the beauty and reverence of these timeless works, the modern viewer is often left in the dark, uncertain of who and what is depicted and, by extension, how to properly engage and appreciate such artwork. However, one figure can always be easily identified: John the Baptist. How? you may ask. By his finger.

Though commonly remembered for his unique diet and dramatic dress, John the Baptist's *finger* is in many ways his most defining feature, for with it, he fulfills his primary role in the story of salvation. John *points* us to Christ, showing us where to go when we are disoriented. He helps us look afresh to Christ when we are confused and cannot see a way forward. In short, he reminds us, often with great passion and urgency, where our focus should be.

In this second week of Advent, we focus on *preparation* and *repentance*. As Isaiah 40:3 reminds us, "In the wilderness prepare the way of the LORD; make straight in the desert a highway for our God." In the busyness of this holiday season, your focus is likely scattered and pulled in a dozen different directions. Yet amid this noise, each year Christians are invited to again tune their hearts to the ancient words of the prophet who proclaimed "a baptism of repentance for the forgiveness of sins" (Mark 1:4). Our Lord is coming. May he find us ready and waiting.

PRAYER *for* THE WEEK

Merciful God, who sent your messengers
the prophets to preach repentance
and prepare the way for our salvation:
Give us grace to heed their warnings
and forsake our sins, that we may greet
with joy the coming of Jesus Christ our
Redeemer; who lives and reigns with
you and the Holy Spirit, one God,
now and for ever. *Amen.*

REFLECTIVE PRACTICE

It's remarkably easy to allow our passions and
desires to pull us in multiple directions. To help guard
against this, we invite you to consider incorporating
the timeless discipline of **fasting** into your rhythm
of life this week.

More specifically, in our perpetually distracted age,
consider fasting from things in your life that contrib-
ute to the "noise" in our lives. What's one thing you
can take a break from this week? A TV show, music
on a car ride, or perhaps a podcast?

Be creative, and keep this truth close to your heart:
when we fast, we say "no" so we can say "yes" to
something better!

NOTES

"Acquire the
Spirit of Peace and
a thousand souls
around you will
be saved."

-St. Seraphim of Sarov

Heavenly Peace

 OPEN DWELL AND LISTEN TO
*Psalm 27; Isaiah 26:7–15;
Acts 2:37–42*

AS COUNTLESS CAROLS, FILMS, AND FAMILY CUSTOMS fill the season, it's easy to pass through these weeks bathed in a warm, nostalgic glow. As we sing each year, "All is calm, all is bright." And while we can joyfully celebrate this season as one of "heavenly peace," we shouldn't too quickly associate this peace with undisturbed tranquility. In truth, the Incarnation of Christ was anything but calm, with earthly powers immediately disturbed and outraged by the birth of this newborn king (Matt 2).

Peace is not the absence of conflict but the presence of God in the midst of chaos. The psalmist reminds us of this, saying, "Though an army encamp against me, my heart shall not fear; though war arise against me, yet I will be confident" (Ps 27:3). The writer knew in his bones something we are daily prone to forget: peace is not circumstantial but given freely by God as a gift. It is, therefore, possible to live in deeply painful and disorienting seasons and remain a person of profound peace.

There is a persistent temptation to tie inner peace to outer calm. And while some chapters of life are simpler or less stressful than others, we can never *guarantee* a life free from all conflict or distress. As Jesus himself reminds us, "In the world you will have tribulation. But take heart; I have overcome the world" (John 16:33)! It does us no good to anxiously worry about the challenges we face in life. Instead, we are invited daily to live free from all fear— not in blind optimism, but deeply rooted in the victory of God won in Jesus.

PRAYER for THE WEEK

Merciful God, who sent your messengers
the prophets to preach repentance
and prepare the way for our salvation:
Give us grace to heed their warnings
and forsake our sins, that we may greet
with joy the coming of Jesus Christ our
Redeemer; who lives and reigns with
you and the Holy Spirit, one God,
now and for ever. *Amen.*

REFLECTIVE PRACTICE

Have you ever noticed the close connection between
hurry and anxiety? The more we busily rush from one
place to the next, the easier it is to be filled with worry.

Are there simple ways you can fast from hurry today?

This doesn't have to be dramatic. Little victories are
to be celebrated! If you share a meal with others, see if
you can be the last to finish. If making a purchase in a
store, intentionally choose the longest line. Slow down,
be present in the moment, and resist the urge to rush
to the next thing!

NOTES

"For that which He has not
assumed He has not healed;
but that which is united to
His Godhead is also saved."

-St. Gregory of Nazianzus

All Things New

 OPEN DWELL AND LISTEN TO
Psalm 27; Isaiah 4:2–6;
Acts 11:1–18

REPENTANCE IS A REMINDER that God loves to heal that
which is sick and restore all that is disfigured. If there is no
possibility for renewal, then why bother with repentance in
the first place? To repent is to acknowledge one's sins and
shortcomings and look ahead with hope and belief that
God will not leave us as we are. He will make us, by grace,
what Jesus is by nature.

In fact, this is one of the most helpful ways to reflect on the
Incarnation during this Advent season. Jesus did not enter
our world because he was lonely; neither was he forced to
do so by some divine decree. *Love* has been and always will
be the only lens through which the birth of Christ can be
properly understood. To truly love is to desire the good of
the other. When God sees humanity suffering and lost in
sin, he looks on us with compassion, longing to free us
from the "sin which clings so closely" (Heb 12:1).

Through our love of self and pursuit of comfort, we walk in
alienation from God and one another. Like the Israelites of
old, we are covered in filth, and our hands are stained with
blood (Isa 4:4). Harsh as it may sound, this realization is
the beginning of true repentance. Only when we see our
sickness for what it is can we begin to appreciate the
healing medicine our loving Lord offers us.

PRAYER for THE WEEK

Merciful God, who sent your messengers
the prophets to preach repentance
and prepare the way for our salvation:
Give us grace to heed their warnings
and forsake our sins, that we may greet
with joy the coming of Jesus Christ our
Redeemer; who lives and reigns with
you and the Holy Spirit, one God,
now and for ever. *Amen.*

REFLECTIVE PRACTICE

As today's reflection reminds us, we are on a
journey toward freedom from the love of self.
In light of this, choose today to fast from
self-interest.

It has been said that true humility is not
thinking less of yourself, but thinking about
yourself less. Here's one tangible way you might
put this idea into practice. Can you go the entire
day without looking at yourself in a mirror?

NOTES

"Idleness is
the enemy
of the soul."

-Rule of St. Benedict

Ready and Waiting

 OPEN DWELL AND LISTEN TO
*Psalm 27; Malachi 2:10–3:1;
Luke 1:5–17*

IF YOU'VE EVER HOSTED GUESTS FOR A MEAL, you know
the routine. For hours before their arrival, you diligently
prepare the food, meticulously clean your home, and make
yourself ready to welcome them when they arrive. If you
succeed, all of this will *appear* effortless, as though you
just happened to throw it all together at the last minute!
The aim is to be ready and *waiting*. With the preparation
and hard work behind you, all that is left is to turn your
attention fully to the guest of honor.

In many ways, Advent is the cooking and cleaning that
must be done to properly welcome our guest. This is not
work for work's sake, busyness just to be busy, or a super-
ficial concern with appearance. No, it is paradoxically the
path to true freedom and rest. When proper preparations
are made, we can live with a *singular* focus and devotion,
not concerned with the weight of the world or the duties
of our lives.

Preparing our hearts and minds allows us to attend to
Christ at his coming. We lay aside all earthly cares to offer
him our full attention and devotion. Do not mistakenly
conflate busyness with faithfulness or idleness with
peace of soul. We must learn to be perfectly at rest while
remaining fully attentive. Only then, in the words of Luke 1,
will we be "a people prepared for the Lord" (Luke 1:17).

PRAYER *for* THE WEEK

Merciful God, who sent your messengers
the prophets to preach repentance
and prepare the way for our salvation:
Give us grace to heed their warnings
and forsake our sins, that we may greet
with joy the coming of Jesus Christ our
Redeemer; who lives and reigns with
you and the Holy Spirit, one God,
now and for ever. *Amen.*

REFLECTIVE PRACTICE

It is impossible to focus on Christ and judge
others at the same time!

Consider ways today to fast from gossip, resisting the urge to speak ill of your brother or sister.
Instead, when you feel tempted to voice your criti-
cism, offer up this simple breath prayer that comes
to us from St. Ephrem: "Help me to see my own
faults and not to judge my brother or sister."

NOTES

"Do not be surprised that you fall every day; do not give up, but stand your ground courageously."

-St. John Climacus

Keep Watch

 OPEN DWELL AND LISTEN TO
Psalm 126; Habakkuk 2:1-5;
Philippians 3:7-11

IN YESTERDAY'S REFLECTION, we spoke of the necessity
of attentiveness, faithfully waiting for our Lord to arrive.
To extend this image further, what do we do when our guest
seems delayed? Do we eat without him? Do we anxiously
call or repeatedly send messages asking for an update?
Perhaps we cancel the meal entirely and head to bed.
Rarely do we do the one thing we are supposed to do:
keep on looking!

The inability to patiently wait and trust the Lord's timing
has plagued his people from the very beginning. What did
the Israelites do when Moses was delayed on Mount Sinai?
They took matters into their own hands and made a golden
calf to worship as a god (Exod 32). What do we do when our
expectations and God's timing seem out of sync? So often, we
quickly assume God to be either uninvolved or uninterested in
the cares and concerns of life and, therefore, believe we must
become masters of our own destiny.

Extended seasons of waiting allow impatience, weariness,
and even bitter resentment to take root in our hearts and
lives. It's a daily struggle to keep watch amid such great
pain and sorrow, and we often fail. Yet, Advent is not a time
to dwell on our failures but to rejoice in the goodness and
faithfulness of God. Hard as it may be, we press on courageously, looking for the day when God will finally set the
world right. As he promises through the prophet Habakkuk,
"(If that final day) seems slow, wait for it; it will surely
come; it will not delay." (Hab 2:3).

PRAYER for THE WEEK

Merciful God, who sent your messengers
the prophets to preach repentance
and prepare the way for our salvation:
Give us grace to heed their warnings
and forsake our sins, that we may greet
with joy the coming of Jesus Christ our
Redeemer; who lives and reigns with
you and the Holy Spirit, one God,
now and for ever. *Amen.*

REFLECTIVE PRACTICE

One of the things that Advent teaches us is just
how hard it is to wait. This can be seen at a macro
level and in the tiny margins of daily life. Since
we struggle to wait, we often fill our "in-between
moments" with stimulation, simply to help us
pass the time.

Instead of mindlessly scrolling or any other
form of potential escape, what if you instead
lift your head, look around, and breathe deeply,
taking in the people and places that are right
in front of you?

NOTES

"As the Wise Men offered
him gifts from their treasure
chests that were mystical
symbols, let us too draw
forth gifts worthy of God
from within our hearts.
He is without a doubt
the giver of all good,
yet he desires the fruits
of our labors."

-St. Leo the Great

Like Those Who Dream

 OPEN DWELL AND LISTEN TO
Psalm 126; Habakkuk 3:2–6;
Philippians 3:12–16

DREAMS, BY THEIR VERY NATURE, have an unobtainable quality. This is what differentiates them from tasks or goals. No amount of careful planning or skill acquisition can guarantee the success of a dream. The vision is simply too big, the hopes too grand. Therefore, if and when a dream *does* come to pass, we can barely contain our sense of amazement or the depths of our wonder. Such moments give birth to the phrase "never in my wildest dreams!"

Psalm 126 is one such moment in the life of Israel. "When the LORD restored the fortunes of Zion, we were like those who dream" (Ps 126:1). As a people suffering under the weight of exile, Israel could never redeem their story or reclaim their future. Yet, in Scripture, we encounter the extravagant love of God extended to helpless people in great need. What Israel could not do for themselves, God did (Rom 8:3). The restoration of their fortunes was nothing short of a dream come true. It is no different for us.

The birth of Christ is a dream we didn't even know to dream. It's a love so selfless no human could possibly imagine it, let alone bring it to pass. It is pure grace, the life of God given for the life of the world. How do we respond to such a remarkable gift? What gift can we possibly offer in return? We offer nothing less than our very lives, poured out in thanksgiving and praise, mouths filled with laughter and tongues that shout for joy (Ps 126:2). These are the gifts we bring the newborn king who has done "far more abundantly than all that we ask or think" (Eph 3:20).

PRAYER for THE WEEK

Merciful God, who sent your messengers
the prophets to preach repentance
and prepare the way for our salvation:
Give us grace to heed their warnings
and forsake our sins, that we may greet
with joy the coming of Jesus Christ our
Redeemer; who lives and reigns with
you and the Holy Spirit, one God,
now and for ever. *Amen.*

REFLECTIVE PRACTICE

During a time of year that is filled with parties
and festive gatherings, it's easy to rush into the
spirit of feasting. Yet, as a season of intentional
preparation, Advent stands in stark contrast to
the cultural themes that surround the holidays.

While avoiding a spirit of rigid self-righteousness,
can you instead with joy choose today to fast from
feasting, avoiding foods typically enjoyed at a
celebratory meal (meat, alcohol, chocolates, etc.)?
Alternatively, consider simplifying the quantity
of food consumed, perhaps cutting out second
helpings or large portions.

NOTES

"When we yield to
discouragement or despair,
it is usually because we
give too much thought to
the past and to the future."

-St. Thérèse of Lisieux

Faithful Obedience

 OPEN DWELL AND LISTEN TO
*Psalm 126; Habakkuk 3:13–19;
Matthew 21:28–32*

THERE STANDS BEFORE US TODAY, and every day, an invitation into faithful obedience. This entry into the way of Jesus is for all who read these words, regardless of where you were yesterday or where you may find yourself tomorrow. Though we may have failed countless times before, the gospel call to repentance can still be heard, received, and obeyed.

In many ways, this is the gift of the Christian year. Advent is an annual reminder and encouragement to renew our commitment to hear and obey the commands of Christ. Though our Lord only once entered this world bodily, *our* need for him to be born anew within us is unending. Like a misaligned car that pulls to the left or right, we humans face a lifelong temptation to deviate from the path that lies before us. We are, as an old hymn says, "prone to wander."

Jesus reminds us in Matthew 21 that faithfulness is found not simply in our words but in and through our lives. The father's will is done by the son who obeys, even though he first resists the father's command. It is not how you begin that defines you but, ultimately, how you finish. As we read yesterday, we must forget what lies behind and instead strain forward to what lies ahead (Phil 3:13). To forget the past is not to pretend it didn't happen but to remove its *power* over your life. In Christ, your past is redeemed and transformed into a glorious future as you faithfully follow him in the present.

PRAYER for THE WEEK

Merciful God, who sent your messengers
the prophets to preach repentance
and prepare the way for our salvation:
Give us grace to heed their warnings
and forsake our sins, that we may greet
with joy the coming of Jesus Christ our
Redeemer; who lives and reigns with
you and the Holy Spirit, one God,
now and for ever. *Amen.*

REFLECTIVE PRACTICE

Fasting is meant to cultivate a hunger for God by
consuming less in other areas of life. To do this,
we must fast from excess, learning to live with less
and allowing our hunger to move us into spaces
of greater fidelity to Christ.

Before we conclude this second week of Advent,
take a few moments today to prayerfully reflect
upon the practices you were able to explore over
the past few days. In what ways did the Lord
reveal something about himself to you? Were there
things you discovered about yourself through
these rhythms of fasting?

NOTES

Third Week *of* Advent

My faithfulness and my steadfast love shall be with
him, and in my name shall his horn be exalted.
Ps 89:24

"Love seeks one thing only:
the good of the one loved.
It leaves all the other
secondary effects to take care
of themselves. Love, therefore,
is its own reward."

-Thomas Merton

Lasting Joy

 OPEN DWELL AND LISTEN TO
Isaiah 61:1-4, 8-11; Psalm 126;
1 Thessalonians 5:16-24; John 1:6-8, 19-28

THIS TIME OF YEAR, gift-giving is top of mind. Likely, you have been busily working through a list, making sure everyone is accounted for and no one slips through the cracks. Similarly, we often call Jesus the "gift of Christmas." Rightly understood, we should celebrate this great truth. However, there is danger before us if we too quickly think of him as a modern Christmas gift, wrapped in the manger and placed gently beneath the tree.

In our culture, Christmas gifts are, by design, not *essential* to our well-being or daily life. In truth, you don't *need* a new gaming console, perfume, or an electric toothbrush, yet these are precisely the types of gifts we give and receive in this season. It's doubtful you will ever wake up on Christmas morning to find a prepaid utility bill wrapped and waiting for you! No, Christmas gifts are meant to do the opposite: they distract from the otherwise difficult and often painful realities of "normal life." As such, though they may bring momentary joy or delight, they rarely bring *lasting* joy or genuine transformation of being.

The gift of God in Jesus is not a momentary fix but a lasting cure. He sees us as we truly are and offers himself as a gift of love to heal our greatest need. Love neither pacifies nor distracts but always renews and restores. Isaiah reminds us of this, pointing to a day of unspeakable joy in which the brokenhearted are restored, mourners consoled, and captives set free (Isa 61:1-3). This is undoubtedly the greatest Christmas gift that could ever be given.

PRAYER for THE WEEK

Stir up your power, O Lord, and with great might come among us; and, because we are sorely hindered by our sins, let your bountiful grace and mercy speedily help and deliver us; through Jesus Christ our Lord, to whom, with you and the Holy Spirit, be honor and glory, now and for ever. *Amen.*

REFLECTIVE PRACTICE

As we take time this week to reflect on the joy of Advent, we must remember that this joy is not simply for our own good. It is a shared joy, one that we receive and extend to others.

Along these lines, this week we will engage the historic practice of **almsgiving,** which in its most basic form is simply showing mercy to others in need. As we prepare for this practice, take time today to reflect on your relationships and spheres of influence. Who will you share life with this week that will present an opportunity to extend the mercy of God in a real or tangible way?

NOTES

"Best of all,
 God is with us."

-John Wesley

God with Us

 OPEN DWELL AND LISTEN TO
Psalm 125; 1 Kings 18:1–18;
Ephesians 6:10–17

JOHN WESLEY DEVOTED HIS ENTIRE LIFE TO GOD, preaching countless sermons, penning well-loved hymns of praise, and inviting everyone around him to live a life of holy devotion to Christ. Yet for all that can be said about his life and ministry, his final words, spoken with great effort as he lay on his deathbed, may be the most important he ever uttered: "Best of all, God is with us."

There are no easy answers to the suffering we see in our world or why God allows such evil to persist. Though we remain a joyful people of hope, we know all is not as it should be. Just as we reflect on the first Advent of Christ in this season, we also long for his return, his Second Advent, praying with Christians through the ages, "Come, Lord Jesus" (Rev 22:20)! The Second Advent reminds us that things will not always be as they are today, and that is very good news. All will one day be made right. Night will give way to day; darkness will yield to the light of Christ. As the psalmist says, "Weeping may linger for the night, but joy comes with the morning" (Ps 30:5).

Joy is found in the presence of God, not in the absence of pain. We are not promised a life free of suffering or loss but are assured that God is with us in these places of great need. As Psalm 125:2 reminds us today, we are surrounded and comforted by a God who is with us and will never leave us: "As the mountains surround Jerusalem, so the LORD surrounds his people, from this time forth and forevermore."

PRAYER for THE WEEK

Stir up your power, O Lord, and with
great might come among us; and,
because we are sorely hindered by our
sins, let your bountiful grace and mercy
speedily help and deliver us; through
Jesus Christ our Lord, to whom, with you
and the Holy Spirit, be honor and glory,
now and for ever. *Amen.*

REFLECTIVE PRACTICE

It's easy to be overcome by the weight of our
own pain and suffering. And, without discount-
ing the reality of our need for healing, if we
are defeated by our own concerns, it becomes
increasingly difficult to give our lives away for the
sake of others.

To help deepen our empathy and turn our hearts
toward others, take time today to call at least
one friend and ask how they are doing and how
you can pray for them this week.

NOTES

"You cannot put straight
in others what is warped
in yourself."
-St. Athanasius

TUESDAY

Shared Joy

 OPEN DWELL AND LISTEN TO
Psalm 125; 2 Kings 2:9–22;
Acts 3:17–4:4

CHRISTIANS OFTEN TALK about living "on mission" or "transforming society" for Christ. And as good and beautiful as these visions are, we must never forget that outer transformation can never move faster than inward renewal. We cannot share with the world something we have not received and encountered in the depths of our souls.

Acts 3 holds forth a vision of refreshment in and through the presence of God, yet it directly ties this refreshment to turning away from sin and towards our Lord in humility. This is the first and primary call of Christ given to every disciple. Though it is clear and easy enough to understand, it is far more difficult to receive and obey. We often prefer to direct the spiritual lives of others rather than tend to our own life with God!

Tempting as this may be, this is not the missional call of God. We are not called to judge others but to give our lives away in service as we seek their good (Matt 7:1). A life free from the power of sin is never for our benefit alone; neither is it meant to isolate us from those in need. Instead, our hearts are set free and are moved by a compassionate longing to enter others' weakness as fellow sinners in need of grace. As we do, the life of God is multiplied in others, and we together enter the joy of our Lord.

PRAYER for THE WEEK

Stir up your power, O Lord, and with great might come among us; and, because we are sorely hindered by our sins, let your bountiful grace and mercy speedily help and deliver us; through Jesus Christ our Lord, to whom, with you and the Holy Spirit, be honor and glory, now and for ever. *Amen.*

REFLECTIVE PRACTICE

Charity requires attentive preparation. We must be ready and eager to give, anticipating the needs of others before they are even known to us.

Today, without any specific need or person on your mind, consider purchasing a few small gift cards from a local gas station or restaurant and place them in your car or bag, and then keep an eye out for ways you might be a blessing to someone in need.

NOTES

"A sure sign of a lukewarm and proud soul is to listen carelessly and negligently to the saving medicine of words which are too zealously and too constantly uttered to it."

-St. John Cassian

Overcome by Joy

 OPEN DWELL AND LISTEN TO
Psalm 125; Malachi 3:16–4:6;
Mark 9:9–13

WHEN WAS THE LAST TIME you were truly overcome by joy? Perhaps it was upon seeing a dearly loved friend or family member after months apart. Maybe it was when you received news of a long-desired promotion or acceptance into the school of your dreams. For others, it was when a prolonged illness found surprising relief and lasting healing. Whatever it may be, this type of joy, one that overpowers and comes upon us with great force, can never be contrived or conjured up. It surprises, overwhelms, and shines light into even the darkest moments of life.

At Christmas, we are meant to be overcome by this kind of joy. The birth of Christ is nothing less than the very life of the world, hope and peace that meets us in our weak and weary state. As Malachi 4:2 reminds us today, "The sun of righteousness shall rise with healing in its wings. You shall go out leaping like calves from the stall."

The joy of the Lord is stronger than your greatest fears. It can handle your greatest doubts. It is saving medicine that cures even the most cynical of souls. And though it comes upon us as a gift, it is a gift that must be accepted. We must open our hearts and lives to receive the saving medicine offered to our sin-sick souls. Let us not neglect the healing we are offered!

PRAYER for THE WEEK

Stir up your power, O Lord, and with
great might come among us; and,
because we are sorely hindered by our
sins, let your bountiful grace and mercy
speedily help and deliver us; through
Jesus Christ our Lord, to whom, with you
and the Holy Spirit, be honor and glory,
now and for ever. *Amen.*

REFLECTIVE PRACTICE

You cannot give to others what you have not first
received. Prayerfully reflect today on the goodness
of God in your life and ask him for the gift of joy
in his presence—and the strength to share that
gift with others.

Throughout your day, keep these words close to your
heart in prayer: "Jesus, give me joy in your presence."

NOTES

"We do not merely want to see beauty, though, God knows, even that is bounty enough. We want something else which can hardly be put into words— to be united with the beauty we see, to pass into it, to receive it into ourselves, to bathe in it, to become part of it."

-C.S. Lewis

THURSDAY

Encountering Beauty

 OPEN DWELL AND LISTEN TO
*Psalm 89:1-4, 19-26; 2 Samuel 6:1-11;
Hebrews 1:1-4*

IN A CULTURE CONSUMED WITH IMAGE AND APPEARANCE,
beauty is almost always thought of as something to *see*
rather than *encounter*. Yet true beauty never leaves us
unaffected, for it is active and engaging, taking hold of
our deepest desires and longings. We are changed and
profoundly affected simply by the presence of beauty, for
all beauty ultimately points beyond itself and invites us
to encounter God as its true source.

Beauty evokes a response, for it is impossible to remain
passive in the presence of beauty. And once we have tasted
it, we will pursue it with all we have. For, within it, we find
our longings awakened and fulfilled. As the psalmist says,
"One thing have I asked of the Lord, that will I seek after:
that I may dwell in the house of the Lord all the days of
my life, to gaze upon the beauty of the Lord" (Ps 27:4).

In Jesus, the beauty of God is on full display. His mercy
and kindness are neither distant nor abstract but can be
known, touched, and encountered. No longer do we hear
and see from a distance as our ancestors did; instead,
God speaks to us through his Son, who is "radiance of the
glory of God and the exact imprint of his nature" (Heb 1:3a).
In Jesus, we encounter the "one thing" the psalmist sought
after: the beauty of God. May we dwell with Christ as he
transforms us daily with the beauty of his love.

PRAYER for THE WEEK

Stir up your power, O Lord, and with great might come among us; and, because we are sorely hindered by our sins, let your bountiful grace and mercy speedily help and deliver us; through Jesus Christ our Lord, to whom, with you and the Holy Spirit, be honor and glory, now and for ever. *Amen.*

REFLECTIVE PRACTICE

While financial gifts are a wonderful way to support people in need, they can never replace the gift of being face-to-face with others. Today, give the gift of your time and physical presence to someone in need, someone who would be blessed simply to have you listen to their story and remind them that they are dearly known and loved by God.

NOTES

"Ultimately, we understand that he became man of a virgin so that the disobedience that started with the serpent would be stopped through the very same path by which it began."

-St. Justin Martyr

The New Eve

 OPEN DWELL AND LISTEN TO
Psalm 89:1–4, 19–26; 2 Samuel 6:12–19;
Hebrews 1:5–14

IN MANY WAYS, the Advent and Christmas seasons can be
understood through the story of two births: Eve, who gave
birth to death and sin, and Mary, who gave birth to life and
hope. In both stories, we encounter a virgin woman living
in the favor of God, each presented with a situation that
demanded a response. For one, it was the temptation to
forcefully seize what can only be given as a gift. For the
other, it was an announcement received with great joy and
trust in the faithfulness of God. As such, while Eve is the
mother of humanity that ushered sin into the world, Mary,
through her "yes" to God, becomes the mother of our Lord
and the true mother of us all.

The journey from Eve to Mary, understood through this
lens, is one that every Christian must take. Through her
response of faith, Mary models how we also must respond
as God draws near. In this way, Mary is one of the pivotal
players of the Advent season, embodying the hopes of Israel
as she receives and proclaims the faithfulness of God.

Today we read Psalm 89, which is an inspiration for the
Song of Mary found in Luke 1. "I will sing of the steadfast
love of the Lord, forever; with my mouth I will make
known your faithfulness to all generations" (Ps 89:1).
Every follower of Jesus is invited to receive the word of
God spoken to them, rejoice in his faithfulness, and
proclaim his goodness to future generations. Though we,
like Eve, have alienated ourselves from our source of life,
with Mary, we even more powerfully magnify the Lord
and rejoice in God our Savior.

PRAYER *for* THE WEEK

Stir up your power, O Lord, and with great might come among us; and, because we are sorely hindered by our sins, let your bountiful grace and mercy speedily help and deliver us; through Jesus Christ our Lord, to whom, with you and the Holy Spirit, be honor and glory, now and for ever. *Amen.*

REFLECTIVE PRACTICE

Every person has a God-given talent that can be used to uniquely support and encourage others. What skill do you have that can bless someone today? Though caring for the poor is a central act of Christian charity, we can also extend the love of God to others in countless ways, such as tutoring children, fixing a leaky pipe, or designing a website.

NOTES

"If he was not flesh, who was lying in the manger? And if he was not God, whom did the Angels come down and glorify? If he was not flesh, who was wrapped in swaddling clothes? And if he was not God, whom did the shepherds worship?"

-St. Ephraim the Syrian

The Mystery of Christ

 OPEN DWELL AND LISTEN TO
Psalm 89:1–4, 19–26; Judges 13:2–24;
John 7:40–52

FAMILIARITY BREEDS CONTEMPT, or so the saying goes. Perhaps you have found this to be true in your own life and close relationships as you struggle to maintain the same level of trust, respect, and intimacy you once had. As broken and sinful creatures, this struggle is real and understandable, yet we must be wary of seeing our life with Christ through a similar lens. Anytime we believe we have exhausted our understanding of Jesus, it is undoubtedly our shortcomings, not his, with which we must contend.

Greater familiarity with Christ should simultaneously awaken us to our need *and* deepen our awareness of the goodness and mercy of God. Only when we try to fit Jesus neatly into our pre-determined categories do we fall into the trap of familiarity: assuming we know all that can be known (or, perhaps more honestly, all that we *want* to know). We face a persistent temptation to reimagine God in our own image. However, true discipleship is always found in our transformation into *his* life and likeness.

Advent plunges us into the depths of the mystery of Christ, fully God and fully man, able to identify with us in our humanity in every way yet uniquely deserving of our praise and adoration. The crowd in John 7 wanted to set the terms and manage their expectations of what and who the Messiah would be. And as tempting as this may be for us, as well, we must remember that true joy is found in a humility and power that is more glorious than anything we could possibly imagine!

PRAYER for THE WEEK

Stir up your power, O Lord, and with great might come among us; and, because we are sorely hindered by our sins, let your bountiful grace and mercy speedily help and deliver us; through Jesus Christ our Lord, to whom, with you and the Holy Spirit, be honor and glory, now and for ever. *Amen.*

REFLECTIVE PRACTICE

As the name implies, there is a proactive reality to almsgiving. It is a gift we give to those in need. However, sometimes the gift is found in our use of restraint and self-control, especially as it relates to things not going our way. Today, give the gift of not having the final word. As you give up your preferences and need for control, you create space for others to shine through, dignifying their personhood and perspective in the process.

NOTES

Fourth Week *of* Advent

And his mercy is for those who fear him
from generation to generation.
Lk 1:50

"Mary was comparing these things which she had read were to occur with those which she recognized as already having occurred. Nevertheless she did not bring these things forth from her mouth but kept them closed up in her heart."

-The Venerable Bede

Ponder These Things

 OPEN DWELL AND LISTEN TO
2 Samuel 7:1–11, 16; Psalm 89:1–4, 19–26;
Romans 16:25–27; Luke 1:26–38

DO YOU HAVE A PRIVATE LIFE with God? As we increasingly live every aspect of our lives on display, posted far and wide for the world to see, it becomes difficult to retain a *hidden* self, especially in a true and redemptive sense. We may be quick to hide things that cause us shame or guilt, yet do we know how to cultivate a life of holy silence and solitude, learning to hear the voice of God as we do?

With Christmas just a few days away, everything in your life is likely ramping up. Nothing about this week feels settled, calm, or quiet! Yet this final week of Advent invites us to resist that chaotic impulse toward anxious hurry and instead listen *and reflect* on the Word of God given to us.

As Mary cultivated the life of a faithful follower of God, including regular times of private prayer and devotion, she found herself present, attentive, and therefore ready to receive the Word of God. Yet as this Word drew near, we see today that it left her disoriented, overcome by its weight and glory. What does she do? She ponders it in her heart (Luke 1:29; see also Luke 2:19). This Advent, the Lord draws near, speaking words of hope and love over his people. Resist the urge to fill the day with endless activities and external concerns, choosing instead to receive and prayerfully ponder the Word of God spoken to you.

PRAYER *for* THE WEEK

Purify our conscience, Almighty God,
by your daily visitation, that your Son
Jesus Christ, at his coming, may find
in us a mansion prepared for himself;
who lives and reigns with you, in the
unity of the Holy Spirit, one God,
now and for ever. *Amen.*

REFLECTIVE PRACTICE

As we enter this fourth and final week of Advent,
each day brings its own unique practice, inviting
us into heightened anticipation and preparation
for the glory of Christmas Day.

Today, you are invited to ponder God's word
to you through silence and solitude, building on
our practice from the first week. Today, seek out
at least 5 minutes of uninterrupted and
undistracted time with God: no people, no screens,
no agenda. Simply be present to God and the
work of the Spirit within you.

NOTES

"Each one of us shapes his soul into the image of Christ and makes either a larger or smaller image of him. The image is either dingy and dirty, or it is clean and bright and corresponds to the form of the original."

-Origen

Magnify the Lord

 OPEN DWELL AND LISTEN TO
*Luke 1:46b–55; 1 Samuel 1:1–18;
Hebrews 9:1–14*

AS WE ENTER THE FINAL DAYS of our Advent journey,
we arrive today at one of the most beloved hymns of
praise in all of Scripture, the Magnificat. Here, with the
Psalms and the Song of Hannah on her heart and mind,
Mary embodies the hopes and dreams of all Israel: "My
soul magnifies the Lord, and my spirit rejoices in God my
Savior" (Luke 1:46-47). As we hear and receive these words
thousands of years later, what does it mean for us to do the
same? How do we, with Mary, magnify the Lord?

Throughout the ages, Christians have often referred to
the *reflective* quality of the human soul. At our best, we are
meant to reflect the life of God in and through the way we
live our lives. This is the aim and goal of every human life,
for each of us is an icon and image bearer of God. Yet, as we
are transformed by his love, we are not simply images to
behold but windows that open to a vast horizon beyond—or,
perhaps more helpfully, mirrors that reflect the light of God
with glorious clarity.

One of the chief effects of sin upon the soul is that it dark-
ens and dirties that mirror, removing our ability to live
lives that magnify the Lord. Is Mary an end or destination
in and of herself? Of course not. Yet, through a life of
faithful living, obedience to God, and openness to his call
on her life, does the Lord clean the mirror of her soul and
shine brightly through her witness in every generation?
Undoubtedly! May we, like her, live lives that magnify and
"image" God in and through our lives, for his glory and the
salvation of the world.

PRAYER for THE WEEK

Purify our conscience, Almighty God,
by your daily visitation, that your Son
Jesus Christ, at his coming, may find
in us a mansion prepared for himself;
who lives and reigns with you, in the
unity of the Holy Spirit, one God,
now and for ever. *Amen.*

REFLECTIVE PRACTICE

Though we all begin our journey of faith
weighed down and darkened by sin, as we
walk with the Lord, he is faithful to cleanse
the mirror of our souls, freeing us to reflect
his light.

Today, take time to look back on the past
year. How has God been present to you
in your joy? How has he consoled you in
your pain?

NOTES

"The Self-revealing of the Word is in every dimension — above, in creation; below, in the Incarnation; in the depth, in Hades; in the breadth, throughout the world. All things have been filled with the knowledge of God."

-St. Athanasius

Filling All Things

 OPEN DWELL AND LISTEN TO
Luke 1:46b–55; 1 Samuel 1:19–28;
Hebrews 8:1–13

ONE OF THE MOST BEAUTIFUL PRAYERS of the ancient church reminds us that God is "everywhere present and filling all things." There is not a single spot in creation left unaffected or untouched by the glory of God; neither is there a corner of the human heart that does not long for God and to live in the light of his love. God's love extends into every part of the world, and as St. Paul reminds us, he is reconciling it—and us—to himself (2 Cor 5:9).

The author of Hebrews, quoting from Jeremiah, reminds us today that God has long promised to fill the hearts and lives of his people. As God reveals himself to his creation, he does so by filling it with his very presence, and this great promise is uniquely fulfilled in the birth of Jesus Christ. How, one might ask, does God go about writing his law "on their hearts" (Heb 8:10)? Though couched in legal language, this is fundamentally a promise of intimacy, a promise of communion. "And they shall not teach, each one his neighbor and each one his brother, saying, 'Know the Lord,' *for they shall all know me*, from the least of them to the greatest" (Heb 8:11).

Jesus enters the brokenness of our existence so that we can know God in the depths of our being. He fills all things so that we can find our fulfillment and true home in him. As St. Irenaeus famously said, "The glory of God is man fully alive." Christ's birth reminds us afresh that we become truly and fully alive as we encounter God's glory in *all* of life.

PRAYER for THE WEEK

Purify our conscience, Almighty God,
by your daily visitation, that your Son
Jesus Christ, at his coming, may find
in us a mansion prepared for himself;
who lives and reigns with you, in the
unity of the Holy Spirit, one God,
now and for ever. *Amen.*

REFLECTIVE PRACTICE

The Incarnation reminds us that God loves our
physical world and will redeem us, soul and body.
As a reminder of the glory of God that fills all
things, take time today to rejoice in creation,
giving thanks to God for the countless ways it
speaks his name and draws forth praise.

NOTES

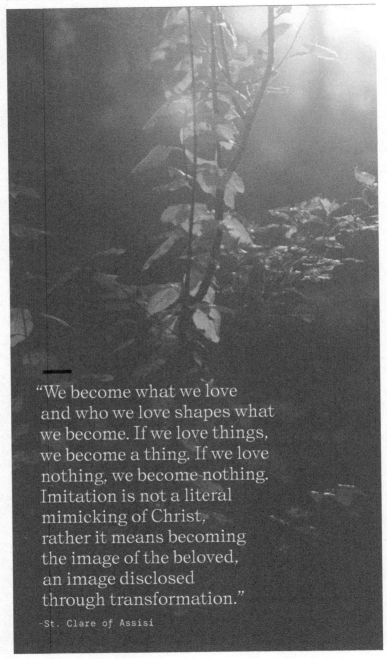

"We become what we love
and who we love shapes what
we become. If we love things,
we become a thing. If we love
nothing, we become nothing.
Imitation is not a literal
mimicking of Christ,
rather it means becoming
the image of the beloved,
an image disclosed
through transformation."

-St. Clare of Assisi

A Triumphal Entry

 OPEN DWELL AND LISTEN TO
Luke 1:46b–55; 1 Samuel 2:1–10;
Mark 11:1–11

AS WE ARE JUST A FEW DAYS AWAY from Christmas, it may feel strange to dive into Mark 11 and the Triumphal Entry of Christ. You may be wondering if the assigned readings were mixed up and misplaced, and at first glance, this is a fair assumption. That said, there is, in fact, profound wisdom in sitting with this story today, for it reminds us that Advent, like the Triumphal Entry, is the story of an approach and an entrance.

As Jesus approached Jerusalem, he was surrounded by people with clear expectations of who he was and was *not* meant to be as a leader. In Jewish minds, he was a political revolutionary, triumphantly entering to overthrow Rome and restore Israel to its rightful place of privilege and power. Yet, just as his entry into Jerusalem shapes and informs our understanding of his birth, the humility of Bethlehem must remind us of the nature of his rule and reign. The babe in the manger is the newborn king who has come to free his people, yet he does so not by force or might but through the humility and self-giving love of the cross.

And so, at both Christmas and Easter, the approach of God in Jesus shines a light on the things we love and hold most dear. What does the birth of Christ reveal within you? How does it shine a light on your truest loves and deepest affections? It is easy to love a version of God that conveniently conforms to all our wants and desires. As verse 8 says, "*Many* spread their cloaks on the road" (Mark 11:8). Many people will have Christ on their minds this week. The question before us is whether we will allow him to transform our loves, desires, *and* assumptions, becoming like him as we do.

PRAYER for THE WEEK

Purify our conscience, Almighty God,
by your daily visitation, that your Son
Jesus Christ, at his coming, may find
in us a mansion prepared for himself;
who lives and reigns with you, in the
unity of the Holy Spirit, one God,
now and for ever. *Amen.*

REFLECTIVE PRACTICE

The way we spend our money is often one of the
clearest indicators of what we truly love. To have
our love transformed by the love of God, we must
first identify places of misdirected desire.

Not as a source of condemnation or guilt, but simply to help us grow in awareness of potential areas
of misalignment, take a simple audit of your spend-
ing over the past week, noting where your funds
went and what that might say about the things
you love most dearly.

NOTES

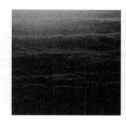

Days Around Christmas Day

He will judge the world in righteousness,
and the peoples in his faithfulness.
Ps 96:13b

"The humbleness
of the heart comes
ahead of all virtues."
-St. Moses the Black

Humble and Lowly

 OPEN DWELL AND LISTEN TO
Psalm 96; Zephaniah 3:8-13;
Romans 10:5-13

IN ZEPHANIAH 3:8, WE AGAIN HEAR words that have frequently framed our Advent journey: "Wait for me." Time and time again, the Lord asks his people to wait, resisting the urge to take matters into their own hands and instead trusting that he will act for their good in his perfect timing. Undoubtedly, the Lord's action is decisive, even dramatic, consuming the earth in the fire of his passion (Zeph 3:8). We must remember that his fire consumes our pride and self-sufficiency, not for our shame (Zeph 3:11) but for us to remember who we are truly meant to be.

The birth of the lowly child to the Virgin Mary invites the world to walk the way of humility. In the Incarnation, true power is displayed for all to see and receive into their lives. Christmas reveals to each of us the way we should walk as we choose to embody the lowliness of our Lord by laying down our lives for the good of the other.

When we fail to wait on the Lord, we cave in to our animalistic impulse to dominate and exploit others to get what we want. We believe the lie of scarcity and choose to fend only for ourselves, believing no one else will look out for us or defend our cause. The weak are conquered and dominated, or so we choose to believe. However, as we await our Lord's arrival, we discover afresh the power of lowliness, trusting that our humble king leads us into places of rest, where "none shall make them afraid" (Zeph 3:13).

PRAYER for THE WEEK

Purify our conscience, Almighty God,
by your daily visitation, that your Son
Jesus Christ, at his coming, may find
in us a mansion prepared for himself;
who lives and reigns with you, in the
unity of the Holy Spirit, one God,
now and for ever. *Amen.*

REFLECTIVE PRACTICE

Hard work is honorable, yet when it turns
into desperation and ceaseless striving, we
step away from a life of faithful trust and instead
take matters into our own hands, trying to
force and guarantee a specific outcome.

Are there ways this struggle resonates with
you in this season? Take a moment to identify
that struggle, and release it to the Lord in
prayer, asking him to act in his power for
your good and his glory.

NOTES

"Those who profess to be Christ's will be recognized by their actions. For what matters is not a momentary act of professing, but being persistently motivated by faith."

-St. Ignatius of Antioch

The Day Is Near

 OPEN DWELL AND LISTEN TO
Psalm 96; Zephaniah 3:14–20;
Romans 13:11–14

SALVATION IS BOTH A MOMENT AND AN ONGOING JOURNEY.
If we miss this, we will struggle to fully grasp the life of
discipleship the Lord invites us to embody in our daily
habits and actions.

Think, for example, of Noah and his family. Their salvation,
we might call it, definitely began as they entered the ark
and found safety from the chaos that swirled around them
(Gen 6:18). However, the ship of salvation was leading them
to a glorious future, a land in which they would once again
be restored to perfect union with their creator. Salvation
was therefore both a beginning and an end. It is no
different for us.

As Christmas Day draws near, we celebrate the beginning
of the story of salvation with grateful hearts. In the humility and vulnerability of the infant Christ, we see God draw
near to rescue his people. In this sense, Noah's Ark points
us to another ark, a humble manger made for livestock.
Within it, the entire human race is invited to find refuge
and restoration.

We journey together on this great ship, and with hearts
of gratitude, we must learn to live by the direction of its
captain, believing his ways are for our good and healing.
As St. Paul exhorts us, as the light of God draws near,
"let us cast off the works of darkness and put on the armor
of light" (Rom 13:12). In the daily practices of our lives,
we point ahead to our final destination and choose to
live as holy people of the light even as we travel through
these shadowlands.

PRAYER for THE WEEK

Purify our conscience, Almighty God, by your daily visitation, that your Son Jesus Christ, at his coming, may find in us a mansion prepared for himself; who lives and reigns with you, in the unity of the Holy Spirit, one God, now and for ever. *Amen.*

REFLECTIVE PRACTICE

The story of the Old Testament is one of a journey, with the people of God invited to follow the Lord, living faithfully under his rule and reign. Similarly, for us, salvation is not only a single moment but is the entirety of our life with God, from first to final breath.

One practice that helps us to cultivate a biblical imagination is to read the Old Testament in light of the New. Specifically, consider listening to Genesis 6-8 in Dwell, allowing the Incarnation of Jesus to shape and inform your understanding of this story and seeing within it your own lifelong pilgrimage of faith.

NOTES

"Not only is the Word of God indeed truly light, but he is also the giver of light to all whom he infuses with the light of understanding.."

-St. Cyril of Alexandria

Love's Pure Light

 OPEN DWELL AND LISTEN TO
*Isaiah 52:7–10; Psalm 98;
Hebrews 1:1–4; John 1:1–14*

FROM THE BEGINNING, the Jewish people have kept a custom of days beginning in the evening, lasting from sundown to sundown. Christians adapted and continued this tradition, establishing a practice of gathering in prayerful anticipation the night before a significant celebration in their common life. Christmas Eve serves as the most enduring example of this tradition. Whatever your church background may be, you have likely experienced the joy of gathering with others on this holy night, singing hymns of praise by the warmth of candlelight.

In a season in which light and darkness feature heavily, this evening dramatically ushers our journey into its final chapter. As our reading reminds us, "The light shines in the darkness, and the darkness has not overcome it" (John 1:5). Though darkness persists throughout our lives, Christmas is the promise that it will never have the final say or last word. No matter how dark it may be, there is always a light to be found. And not only is the light never overcome, but it reaches us in the darkness and promises that we, too, shall be enlightened by its light.

Jesus Christ is the light of the world, the "true light, which gives light to everyone" (John 1:9). He reaches into the darkness and finds us. He illuminates us and enlightens all that is darkened by sin so that we shine with him. The light of Christ does not embarrass or embitter but exposes places of bondage and oppression so that we are set free. He is "love's pure light," a "radiant beam" coming with healing in his wings. Truly, in the darkness of this night, we look with hope and great anticipation for "the dawn of redeeming grace."

PRAYER for THE WEEK

O God, you have caused this holy night
to shine with the brightness of the true
Light: Grant that we, who have known the
mystery of that Light on earth, may also
enjoy him perfectly in heaven; where with
you and the Holy Spirit he lives and reigns,
one God, in glory everlasting. *Amen.*

REFLECTIVE PRACTICE

Culturally, Christmas Eve often consists
of a cherished meal with family or wrapping
last-minute gifts to place discreetly beneath
the tree. In addition to these customs,
consider keeping vigil this evening with those
you love, perhaps listening to the story of
Christ's birth by candlelight, allowing it to
be the final thought on your heart and mind
as you fall asleep.

NOTES

Christmas Day

Sing to the Lord, bless his name;
tell of his salvation from day to day.
Ps 96:2

"The entire human race had a place, and the Lord about to be born on earth had none. He found no room among men. He found no room in Plato, none in Aristotle, but in a manger, among beasts of burden and brute animals, and among the simple, too, and the innocent."

-St. Jerome

No Room in the Inn

 OPEN DWELL AND LISTEN TO
Isaiah 9:2 7; Psalm 96;
Titus 2:11 14; Luke 2:1 20

IF CHRISTMAS EVE IS AN ENTRY into the glory, wonder, and majesty of the Incarnation, with the hosts of heaven praising God in the highest, then Christmas Day brings with it a certain humility, a homely faith as we gather with the Holy Family in the stable. Jesus Christ is Lord of creation, yet there was no room for him in this world, no place to be found. This is true historically, yet if we have eyes to see and ears to hear, this is a word spoken to our hearts today.

When the inn of our heart is filled to overflowing with arrogance and superiority, self-interest and greed, there is no room for the humble king to enter. Yet enter he will, for he is good and loves us in our blindness, so he goes and makes his home among the animals and the innocent, the pure and lowly of heart. If we want to meet Christ this Christmas, we too must be willing to enter the lowliness of the stable and there find our true home, the way that leads to life.

If you find no room for Christ in the inn, it may be time to leave the inn behind! So often, we are in love with the inn, the creature comforts of this life, and simply wait and hope that Christ will come to us in *that* place of waiting. However, we are never called to wait contently in our sins but are told to *go*, to lay aside the weight of life that clings so closely (Heb 12:1). Yes, at Christmas, Jesus comes to us, but when there is no place in the inn (Luke 2:7), we must boldly go to him.

PRAYER for CHRISTMAS DAY

Almighty God, you have given your only-begotten Son to take our nature upon him, and to be born this day of a pure virgin: Grant that we, who have been born again and made your children by adoption and grace, may daily be renewed by your Holy Spirit; through our Lord Jesus Christ, to whom with you and the same Spirit be honor and glory, now and for ever. *Amen.*

REFLECTIVE PRACTICE

As the classic song reminds us, Christmas is not a single day but a twelve-day feasting season! With the hard work of preparation now behind us, enter the joy and delight of Christmas and keep the feast with those you love, recounting each day the hope we have in Jesus Christ, God with us.

NOTES

Endnotes

Lectionary selections are reprinted from Revised Common Lectionary Daily Readings for Year A, copyright © 2005. Consultation on Common Texts, Augsburg Fortress Publishers. Reproduced by permission.

Scripture quotations are from The ESV® Bible (The Holy Bible, English Standard Version®), copyright © 2001 by Crossway, a publishing ministry of Good News Publishers. Used by permission. All rights reserved.

Prayers are taken from *The Book Of Common Prayer and Administration of the Sacraments and Other Rites and Ceremonies of the Church: Together with the Psalter or Psalms of David According to the Use of the Episcopal Church.* New York: Seabury Press, 1979.

Made in the USA
Las Vegas, NV
11 November 2023

80548572R00075